FIRST
BIOGRAPHIES

P.T. Barnum

Published by Raintree Steck-Vaughn Publishers, an imprint of Steck-Vaughn Company

Planned and produced by The Creative Publishing Company
Editors: Christine Lawrie and Pam Wells

Library of Congress Cataloging-in-Publication Data

Wright, David K.
    P. T. Barnum / David Wright; illustrated by Mike White.
       p.   cm. — (First biographies)
    Summary: Introduces the life and accomplishments of the man who is known as the creator of "the greatest show on Earth."
    ISBN 0-8172-4456-5
    1. Barnum, P .T. (Phineas Taylor), 1810-1891 — Juvenile literature.
2. Circus owners — United States — Biography — Juvenile literature.
[1. Barnum, P. T. (Phineas Taylor), 1810-1891 . 2. Circus owners.]
I. White, Mike (Mike H.), 1939- ill. II. Title. III. Series.
GV1811.B3W75   1997
338.7'.617913' 092 — dcB — dc20   96-20369
                                                     CIP
                                                      AC

Printed and bound in the United States
1 2 3 4 5 6 7 8 9 0 W 99 98 97 96

FIRST
BIOGRAPHIES

P.T. Barnum

David Wright
Illustrated by Mike White

RSVP

RAINTREE
STECK-VAUGHN
PUBLISHERS
The Steck-Vaughn Company

Austin, Texas

Phineas Taylor Barnum was born on a farm in Bethel, Connecticut, in 1810. Like most Americans in the 1820s, he and his family worked from dawn to dusk. There were chores every day with very little time for fun. There were no movies, no television, and not much music outside church.

P. T. did not like the long hours he spent in the fields looking after cattle. He wondered what was life like in the big city. When he was twelve, P. T. was offered a more exciting job. A neighbor needed help driving cattle to New York City. P. T. was dazzled by New York. There were museums, shops, theaters, restaurants, shows, and tall buildings. He went back home but longed to work in a big city.

Instead, P. T. took a job as a store clerk in Bethel. He made extra money by running his own lottery. People paid a small amount hoping to win a prize worth much more. But P. T. used cheap green bottles as prizes. At first, people were angry, yet they admired him for giving away so many prizes!

When he was seventeen, P. T. got a job as a clerk in Brooklyn, New York. He spent his spare time at the theater, where he dreamed of putting on his own shows. He knew the folks back home would be amazed at the tricks and jokes. He married his girlfriend, Charity Hallett, and went home to Connecticut. He was only nineteen years old.

Politics began to interest P. T. He did not approve of slavery, which still existed in those days. The local newspaper would not print his letters protesting it, so P.T. started his own newspaper. But sometimes he wrote stories without finding out all the facts.

Once, he said that a neighbor took an orphan's last cent. It made a good story, but he could not prove it. The neighbor sued P. T. for libel. Libel is saying untrue things in print. P. T. was sent to jail for sixty days. Very soon after this, he gave up the newspaper business.

By 1834, P. T. was back in New York City with his wife and baby daughter. One day, he saw an amazing show. It starred a woman who was said to be 161 years old! Her name was Joice Heth. She was an African-American slave who said she had taken care of George Washington when he was a baby. But no one knew for sure if this was true.

P. T. bought the woman. He also became the manager of a talented Italian juggler called Signor Vivallo. The three went on tour all over the United States in the 1830s. P. T. made sure of large crowds by giving stories to newspapers. In one town he wrote that Joice Heth was a robot! People turned out everywhere to see if what they read was true.

In 1841, Barnum bought the American Museum in New York City, even though he did not have a cent. He promised to give the museum back to its owner if he ever missed a monthly payment. He never did.

When Barnum bought the museum, it was not very exciting. So he brought in live shows. These had nothing to do with the usual things you see in museums. Instead, there were fat men, thin men, very small people, very tall people, sword swallowers, woolly ponies, and many other curious things. People came to stare. They wanted to be amused and shocked — even fooled.

Though he knew it was a hoax, P. T. bought and showed a dead mermaid. He later said the exhibit was half-fish and half-monkey, and it had been glued together in Japan!

FEJEE MERMAID

Barnum made a lot of money from the exhibits in the American Museum. But he spent lots of money, too, and he was often broke. He sometimes bought big meals for newspaper people. He hoped they would write about his shows. P. T. tried all kinds of things to make money. In 1843, he brought a load of buffalo from the West to New Jersey and staged a large buffalo hunt there.

A few years later, he showed off Chang and Eng, two brothers from Thailand who were Siamese twins. They had been born joined together at the chest. Today, people like this would be helped in other ways. But in Barnum's time the only way they could earn money to live was for them to go into a sideshow. The twins and others soon made P. T. rich. In return, he took good care of the people in his shows and paid them well.

The most popular person in Barnum's show was Tom Thumb. Tom's real name was Charles Stratton. When he was four years old, he was just 25 inches high — no taller than an adult's knee!

Tom Thumb was a talented entertainer. He told jokes, danced, sang, and acted in plays. He played to the American president James K. Polk, in 1847. Later, he even appeared before Britain's Queen Victoria at Buckingham Palace. Tom loved Barnum and worked for the showman for over forty years.

By 1850, Barnum was very rich. He returned to Fairfield, Connecticut with his family. He had a huge, fancy home built and called it Iranistan. It looked like a great palace. To help pay for the home, he brought Jenny Lind to America. She was known as "The Swedish Nightingale" because she had a wonderful singing voice.

Barnum also set up "Barnum's Great Asiatic Caravan, Museum, and Menagerie." This was one of the first real circuses, although there were no rings or clowns. However, it did have a herd of elephants and the first live hippopotamus in New York.

While the circus went on tour, Barnum stayed in New York. But he was so busy that he did not have time for the American Museum, and he sold it.

By 1856, Barnum was out of money again. He sold his huge house and went on tour in Europe with Tom Thumb. They did many shows in Britain, France, and Holland. A family called the Howards went with them. The Howards had been slaves. A famous book called *Uncle Tom's Cabin* was about their lives. The book helped President Abraham Lincoln gain support for the Civil War, which ended slavery.

P. T. worked hard in Europe, giving talks on "The Art of Money-Getting" and other subjects. When he got back home, he was able to buy back the American Museum. He loved the big building with its many exhibits. Then, he started another circus that was a great success. In 1867, P. T. ran for a seat in the United States Congress, but he was defeated.

In 1865, the American Museum burned to the ground! Once more P. T. needed money. In 1871, he opened "P. T. Barnum's Museum, Menagerie, and Circus" under a huge canvas tent in Brooklyn.

Then, the show went on tour. At each stop people rushed to the railroad station to see the circus train pull in. A grand parade ran from the train to the place where the huge circus tent was being put up. Schools, stores, and factories emptied so everyone could watch the colorful circus parade go by.

Barnum was the most famous circus manager
of his time. But he was not the only one. To make
his circus even better, he became partners with
James A. Bailey in 1880.

It was hard work keeping the Barnum and Bailey circus "The Greatest Show on Earth." In 1882, Barnum bought Jumbo, a huge African elephant. Jumbo became the talk of the circus world. People were amazed at his size and power. He was so huge that Barnum said he was an ancient prehistoric mastodon! Sadly Jumbo was hit by a train and killed after a show in Ontario, Canada, in 1885.

Barnum had many other animals, including a rare white elephant. Besides the animals, the acrobats, and the clowns, Barnum offered many sideshow stunts. A stunt is an unusual or difficult act. It is often done to get attention. One stunt was "a man-eating chicken." When they went into the sideshow booth, circus-goers soon found out that this was really a man eating a chicken drumstick!

A lot of the best acts from other smaller circuses joined Barnum and Bailey. Soon there were so many acts that the circus had to have three rings — all inside a huge tent nicknamed the Big Top. Three different, exciting acts went on at the same time. And what acts they were! The animals wore fancy harnesses, and the performers wore shiny costumes. The clowns kept people laughing for hours.

Circus life was really very hard work. Circus people traveled during the day and performed at night. But the magic of the Big Top made it all worthwhile.

In 1887, fire swept the winter quarters of the circus in Connecticut. Many animals died in the blaze, including the white elephant. By this time, P. T. Barnum was 77 years old. People thought he might retire. But the next season saw an even bigger and better circus. "The show," Barnum decided, "must go on."

P. T. Barnum died in 1891. The Ringling Brothers bought the Barnum and Bailey Circus in 1906. With its animals, acrobats, clowns, and sideshows, it is still known today as "The Greatest Show on Earth."

Key Dates

1810 Born on July 5, in Bethel, Connecticut.

1829 Marries Charity Hallett in New York City.

1835 Buys Joice Heth, an elderly woman slave who claims to have been George Washington's nanny. They tour the United States with a juggler.

1841 Buys the American Museum in New York City.

1842 The "Fejee Mermaid" proves to be a hoax.
Meets Tom Thumb, the famous dwarf.

1850 Begins a tour with singer Jenny Lind, "The Swedish Nightingale."

1867 Runs for the United States Congress and loses.

1871 "P. T. Barnum's Museum, Menagerie, and Circus" opens in Brooklyn.

1873 Charity Hallett dies. Barnum marries Nancy Fish.

1880 Becomes partners with James A. Bailey.

1891 Dies on April 7.